Crafting Peg Doll Play Sets

Home Accessories

Emily Kellagher

Crafted Joy Press

For more information:

https://craftedjoypress.com

ISBN: 979-8-89316-751-1 - eBook
ISBN: 979-8-89316-752-8 - Paperback

Join our Peg Doll Creative Community

Throughout the book you will see this icon. It has a QR Code link to an online community we are building. Instead of using a social media platform, where the security of your content can change at times, this community is managed by our own press team and so content and data is more secure.

I want to create a space where we can upload pictures of our creations, and share ideas on painting peg dolls and accessories, as well as tips and triumphs. It is free to join! I would love to see your creations!!!

Emily

Contents

Introduction

Inspiration

My grandchildren have inspired me to design, build and create imaginative peg doll play-scapes. I love pretend play and am fortunate enough to be able to play with them often. When we play together, they might mention that they would like a special accessory to enhance the play. "Nana, we need a shopping cart for the store!" Then I will set out to create that for them.

Making simple toys for children is fun, economical and a great way to connect with your child through play. All parents want toys that nurture and develop the creativity and learning ability that children naturally possess. Plain, basic toys are great for child development because they allow children to use their imaginations and create stories or puzzles with the toys. With plain, basic toys, there is no need for batteries or complex instructions, so children can easily engage with the toy. Additionally, these toys encourage creative problem-solving skills, which are essential for cognitive development.

What is a Peg Doll

Peg dolls are simple, small wooden figures that are shaped like a peg, with a rounded head and a cylindrical body. They lack detailed features, which allows for a wide range of imaginative play and creativity. Peg dolls, with their simplistic design have endless potential for customization. They are gender neutral, and can represent people, animals or even fantastical characters, anything a child can think of. The allure of peg dolls lies in their versatility, allowing for a myriad of creative expressions and play scenarios.

Why Wood

Wood is a natural and healthy choice of material for toys. For crafting your own toys, wood is easy to paint and repaint. Wooden toys are generally more durable and can withstand rough play better than plastic toys. They are less likely to break, making them long-lasting.

Another unique aspect of wood peg dolls is that they can be easily customized to fit whatever style or decor you'd like. They have a classic charm but can be painted with a contemporary aesthetic to reflect your style. In addition, wood peg dolls aren't as prone to melting or warping in extreme temperatures like plastic dolls so they travel well in cars and can survive being left outside.

Peg dolls are generally considered safe. The edges are typically sanded smooth to prevent any sharp edges or splinters, and the materials used to make them are non-toxic. However, it's always best to keep an eye on young children when they are playing with any type of toy.

A 12-month-old can play with unpainted 3.5 inch or larger wooden peg dolls. If you're buying these to make for toddlers, just remember that anything that can fit inside of a cardboard tube is a choking hazard. Therefore, you need to buy the larger peg dolls for toddlers.

Easy to Replace

A wonderful aspect of handmade toys is the ease of replacement. Make the toys as carefully as your personality dictates. Artistry and durability are important, but the educational value is not diminished by imperfections. Keep in mind these toys are meant to be used by young hands. Children will scratch, drop or wear them down eventually so you should not worry about trying to keep them pristine (think of the well-loved, well-worn rabbit in the Velveteen Rabbit story). When toys get left behind at the playground or lost in the yard, you can make new ones and if your children are interested, they can even help you design the replacement.

Tip: Children like to make their own dolls. Keep in mind, their goal is to create the doll and go play so their dolls will not have an "adult look" to them. As long as they are satisfied, we should accept these toys as is. A snapshot of childhood joy.

Expandable

As your child grows you can add additional toy accessories. This is great for vocabulary and imagination. You may also incorporate other learning opportunities for math and STEM into play sets.

I created play levels to guide you through the process of creating peg doll accessories. Occasionally adding new accessories and props will revitalize and stimulate a child's play. Remember that adding too many accessories with a younger child can be overwhelming and create a cluttered play environment. That said, you know your child best, so follow your child's lead and add things when they are ready. Start out with a few simple props and when they show interest in different accessories you can add them in.

I offer many other books based on different themes so be sure to check these out with your child and let their interests guide your toy making!

Play Levels

Planning peg doll accessories to add in stages is a nice alternative to buying random, unrelated toys that will only engage your child maybe for a few days after purchase. Your child will naturally invent and expand their play as they grow older so pay attention to their interests and plan together what accessories you can add that will enrich their imagination.

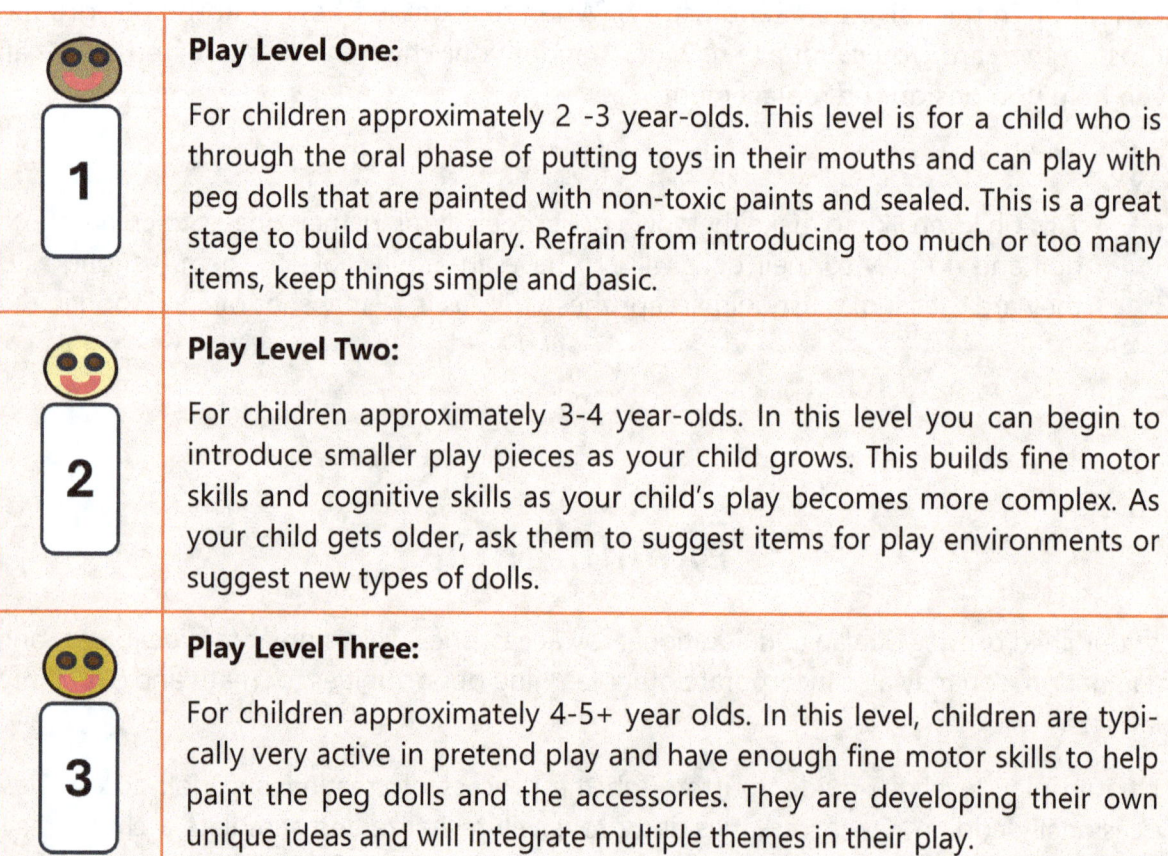

Play Level One:

For children approximately 2 -3 year-olds. This level is for a child who is through the oral phase of putting toys in their mouths and can play with peg dolls that are painted with non-toxic paints and sealed. This is a great stage to build vocabulary. Refrain from introducing too much or too many items, keep things simple and basic.

Play Level Two:

For children approximately 3-4 year-olds. In this level you can begin to introduce smaller play pieces as your child grows. This builds fine motor skills and cognitive skills as your child's play becomes more complex. As your child gets older, ask them to suggest items for play environments or suggest new types of dolls.

Play Level Three:

For children approximately 4-5+ year olds. In this level, children are typically very active in pretend play and have enough fine motor skills to help paint the peg dolls and the accessories. They are developing their own unique ideas and will integrate multiple themes in their play.

The Peg Dolls

Peg Doll Planning

I started our peg doll collection with the 3½ inch dolls (jumbo angel and jumbo male dolls). They are great for younger children who still mouth toys. We started playing with the large dolls. We had a few playscapes, but it seems all children like to start with what is familiar such as rooms of a house. Note the 3½ inch dolls also fit well with commercial doll houses.

We made the accessories to scale with the 3½ inch dolls as the adults. (there is no need to label them as such for your children) As your child grows, they will be thrilled when you add "children" sized dolls (2.5 inch).

Jumbo Angel Doll

females

Jumbo Male Doll

men

Peg doll man

child

Peg Doll Painting

With younger babies that still put toys in their mouths, the large jumbo peg dolls are great for teething. You do not need to paint them, just make sure they are finished smoothly. Then as your child grows, you can just paint the doll base. Start with basic colors for teaching color identification. As your child matures, add details to the dolls, such as hair, faces and more detailed body patterns.

Materials needed

Wood Peg Doll: The various sizes and styles mentioned previously, 3 ½ inch dolls and 2 ½ inch dolls.

Sandpaper: Very fine, 220 Grit. I don't always sand dolls but occasionally I find a doll or two that could use some sanding. I do occasionally make mistakes when painting so having some sandpaper around is handy for sanding off those boo boos.

Paint brushes: Start out with a variety of brushes. Flat brushes apply paint evenly and quickly to blocks of wood. Smaller brushes are great for painting details. I also use tiny dowels the size of toothpicks to paint eyes and dot decorations. I have a few old paint brushes where the bristles have fallen off but the handles work well for painting various size dots on projects.

Planning Sheet

Finishing the Dolls for Durability

The varnish on wooden toys must be safe for little ones. There are nontoxic varnishes on the market that seal the wood effectively and give it an attractive sheen while still being safe in your child's hands. Just be sure to read the label carefully.

Varnishes that fall under the heading of "safe for children's toys" have similar characteristics. These varnishes are water-based. Water-based varnishes don't contain the flammable, and highly toxic ingredients present in oil-based varnishes.

Acrylic Polymer Varnish

Varnishes made with acrylic polymers can be nontoxic. The mixture of water and acrylic gives this varnish a milky appearance, but after you apply it and the water evaporates, the varnish will look clear on the wood. Read labels carefully to choose a pure acrylic product described as nontoxic and VOC-free.

A Thin Coat of Varnish is Enough

Finish each project with one thin coat of varnish. It will create a durable finish with the added advantage of being faster drying than a thick coat. Professional peg doll artists will use multiple coats of varnish so determine what works best for you.

Let Varnish Dry Completely

Let the varnish dry completely before giving the toy to your child to play with. A good 12 -24 hours is generally long enough.

> **Tip:** I use separate brushes for varnishing and painting. And I never let the varnish dry on a brush, it goes into water after each use to be cleaned.

Caring for Your Peg Dolls

While it is fun to imagine my grand-children passing their peg dolls on to their children. I never imagine that they will stay pristine over time, but I do make an effort to minimize the wear and tear that throwing them in the toy bins makes. There are a few things you can do to help preserve your peg dolls. Here are my simple suggestions.

Only protect the dolls with fancy painted details. Plainly painted dolls can easily be refreshed or replaced. I sew little sleeves for our fancy detailed dolls, and during clean up time, we slip each doll into a sleeve and pretend that we are putting the dolls asleep until we play with them again. The sleeves also function as sleeping bags and shopping bags during our playtime. I am amazed that my granddaughter has started to recognize her favorite dolls just

from seeing the bottom of the doll in their sleeve. I have fun with sleeve making, using thematic fabrics to go with the theme of the accessories. See the doll sleeve pattern in the sewing section of the bedroom chapter.

Skills

Projects in this book are mainly focused on being practical and approachable. I always try to make projects as simple as possible. But there are a few design challenges for the intermediate woodworker. I created a simple system for designating which skills are needed for a project. Use these as guides when you decide which projects to try.

	**Basic Sewing:** Machine sewing is most efficient. You will only need straight stitches and basic sewing machine skills. (straight stitch, zigzag stitch, and optional pinking shears)
	**Painting:** You need wood pieces purchased from a craft store or home center to paint.
	**Decoupage:** Mod Podge is great for pieces that require details that are hard to paint. Find copyright free images online to print and use. This allows for your tastes to shine through.
	**Basic Woodworking:** Basic cutting and sanding of wood is needed to accomplish these projects Tools: saw, drill, sanding block.
	**Involved Woodworking Skills:** These projects are made easier with tools such as band saw, handheld router, drill press, and sander. Because you are working with small pieces of wood, you do not need heavy duty tools and many maker spaces at libraries have these tools. You can also request the maker space add tools to their inventory.

Sewing Skills

My goal in this book is not to teach you sewing skills, I want to inspire you and give you options. You can create fun and cute doll bedding and rugs without sewing. Just use the suggested finished sizes as a template for cutting out your projects. If you do know how to sew, I have included sewing patterns as well. I also recommend using cloth from your child's outgrown clothes or other clothing that can be used for projects. Children love seeing the material of a beloved piece of clothing become something new to play with!

No Sewing Required

Making items for your dolls is fun and rewarding especially when your child can help and create with you. Using felt and fabric paint requires no sewing skills and felt is very durable. Consider using pinking shears when cutting out room rugs to make the edges a little fancier.

Fleece is also a great option for doll bedding since fleece also does not fray and it is very soft, kids love it!

Basic Sewing Tips

If you decide to try sewing some accessories, look for fabrics with tighter weaves, such as quilting cotton or tightly woven blends. These fabrics tend to be more durable and less susceptible to fraying, making them ideal for peg doll projects. Fleece is a great option for doll bedding. I have even cut up old fleece blankets, using the less worn parts to make several doll blankets.

No Hemming Option

You hem material to have a nice, finished edge but also to keep fabric from fraying

Seam sealants, such as fray check or fabric glue, can be applied to fabric edges to prevent fraying. Another tool that can help prevent fraying is pinking shears. These specialized scissors have zigzag-shaped blades that create a serrated edge when cutting fabric. The zigzag pattern helps minimize fraying by reducing the length of the fabric threads that are exposed. My favorite pinking shears have scalloped edges.

Stitching

All projects use a basic straight stitch but feel free to embellish using a zigzag stitch when you are top stitching.

· · ·

Woodworking Skills – Basic Cuts

 I have basic middle school woodworking class skills. I know how to measure and use basic tools safely. I initially used the tools at my community maker space. Eventually when I decided that creating accessories for the peg dolls was something that I wanted to do on a regular basis, I invested in what I consider more advanced tools such as a band saw and drill press. Most community maker spaces give lessons on using these tools. This will also help you decide if you want to invest in some tools of your own. Since most of these projects are small, you do not need industrial quality tools which can be expensive. See the resource list for the type of tools I use.

Just Gluing

Many of the projects only require gluing precut wood together. Use a wood glue that dries clear. Use the project patterns to see placement of pieces.

Making Cuts

I make all my cuts on a band saw these days, but when I started out, I used Japanese saws. These are super sharp hand saws that come in smaller sizes that are perfect for cutting dowels and straight lines in boards, especially quarter inch hobby boards.

The Project Process

Measure: I give the exact size of the items I made but really there is room for customization. So if you are off by an eight or quarter inch, it will not really impact any of the basic woodworking projects.

Cut: Cut with care, using tools safely.

Sand: Always sand wood to smooth surfaces and round the edges for safer play. Tactilely, projects feel better to play with when sanded smooth.

Finish: See the section on finishing peg dolls, use your preferred method on the wood accessories as well.

· · ·

Advanced Woodworking Skills

 Projects that require advanced woodworking skills, involve cutting several pieces of wood that will be glued together, drilling specific sized holes on projects and / or cutting shapes with curves. You will also find projects where I suggest using a sander to create a smooth even curve as well and I consider this a little more advanced. I do not consider these projects "hard" they just may require a bit more time and thoughtfulness.

Advanced Woodworking Tools

After years of toy making, I invested in some basic tools that make toy making quick and easy for me. I consider a bandsaw to be the best upgrade I made. A drill press stand, or a small drill press helps improve precision and makes quick work of adding holes to wood for your projects. Two tools that are not essential but help you to quickly have nice smooth edges on projects are a hand router and a spindle sander.

See Resource page for tool suggestions.

· · ·

Let's Create

 Children recognize themselves and their families, friends and pets in play figures. Playing with them helps them consolidate their understanding of the world, from driving a car to cooking in the kitchen. Children love to have just the right figure for their small world play, but it's not essential. Their imaginations will fill in the gaps. Listening and playing with your child will guide what accessories to create and add to their play.

If your child doesn't know how to pretend yet you might need to start off the play. Pick up a toy your child likes and do one simple action yourself to give your child the idea. **Keep it simple.** There's no need to introduce too many new pretend ideas at once. Children love repetition and learn from it, so they will likely enjoy practicing any new pretend actions over and over again. Start with creating the play level one accessories and then add level two and three based on your child's interests.

A good place to start is the Basic Rooms of a house. In level one play, the kitchen and bedroom come first. A bathroom is still an adult concept (except maybe for a bathtub) since the child themselves may still be in diapers. But as they start to be interested in sinks and toilets you can add these to your play. Level one play should be child safe where no objects pose a choking hazard.

Level two play will start to introduce more detailed play items and often smaller pieces so introduce these items when it is safe to do so. Adding too many new toys at once can be overwhelming to some children. So, select a few key additions that you think your child may like.

You can continue to model pretend scenarios, with the new additions. There is no need to rush to level two play. You will notice when your child's pretend play starts to expand beyond the toys you have. This is your signal to add a few more accessories.

At level three play, your child will start to direct the play and will start to come up  with ideas for themes such as playing Zoo or shopping. You can also suggest items and themes and together have lots of fun!

Start with a Bedroom

Play Level Guide for Building and Expanding Doll Bedrooms

1

Level 1:

Bed and Bedding

2

Level 2:

Bed (from level 1),
Bedding (from level 1)
Add: Nightstand

3

Level 3:

Bed (from level 1),
Bedding (from level 1),
Nightstand (from level 2)
Add: Lamp, Radio

Beds

Beds are one of the first pieces of furniture to add to your play. Bedtime and naptime are pretty important in a young child's life, and they instantly understand that their dolls need to rest too.

I was lucky to find some inexpensive wood soap dishes that make terrific doll beds. Later, when we needed more beds, I ended up making some basic beds instead of spending time hunting for more soap dishes.

If you find some nice inexpensive wood soap dishes, by all means load up but another no build method is to buy some wooden plaques at the craft store!

I also have an inexpensive and practical method to build your own double and single doll beds!

You can leave the beds unpainted or paint them in bright colors. See the bedding patterns to add your own blankets and sleeping bags to the beds.

Simple No Build Bed

Want a quick bed for your dolls? Use these inexpensive wood plaques. All you need to do is paint them and they are ready to go. An added bonus, your dolls will never fall out of bed!

Materials needed:

3" wood unfinished plaque See resource page for stores who carry this.
Painting supplies: Paint of choice, brushes, water to clean brush

Steps:

1. Paint the plaque as you desire.
2. Note: if you plan to add a mattress you could leave the inside unfinished.
3. Apply clear coat to painted areas.
4. Allow clear coat to fully dry before you begin playing.

See how to create a mattress and bedding for this bed in the Sewing Bedroom Accessories section.

Build a Bed

Making your own beds is a way to customize your house and, it can be, more efficient than searching for the right soap dish.

The following pages have instructions for single and double beds that you can make. You will need to cut some wood to size and glue them together. They are also projects that can be made with basic woodworking skills.

You can leave the beds unpainted or paint them.

See the bedding patterns to add your own blankets and sleeping bags to the beds in the Sewing Bedroom Accessories section.

Double Bed

Materials Needed:

2 - 4" square coaster
2 ¼ " square dowel cut to 4"
Wood glue

Steps:

1. Cut one of the 4" coasters in half.
2. Sand your cut edges smooth.
3. Wipe all surfaces with dry cloth to clean.
4. Make the head and foot boards by measuring and marking ½ inch from the cut edge of a half coaster.

5. Glue one ¼ inch square dowel to each half coaster along the mark you just made.

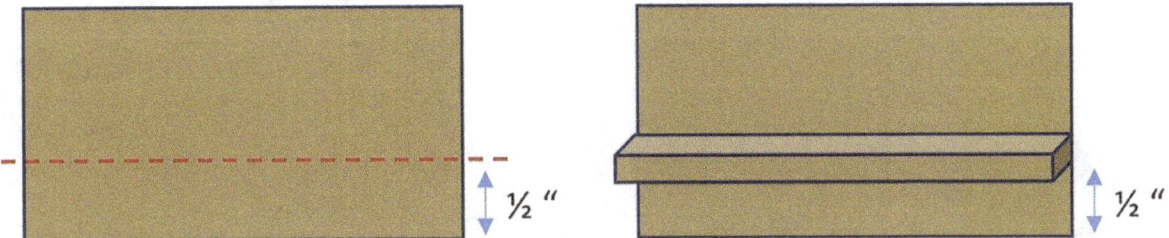

6. Gently clean off any excess glue, and let dry fully.
7. Glue the 4" square coaster to the head and foot boards, resting on the ¼ inch square dowel.
8. Gently clean off any excess glue.
9. Hold bed together for a few minutes to let the glue start to set.
10. Once the glue is dry, apply paint (optional), and let dry fully.
11. Apply clear coat (optional).
12. Let dry fully before you begin playing.

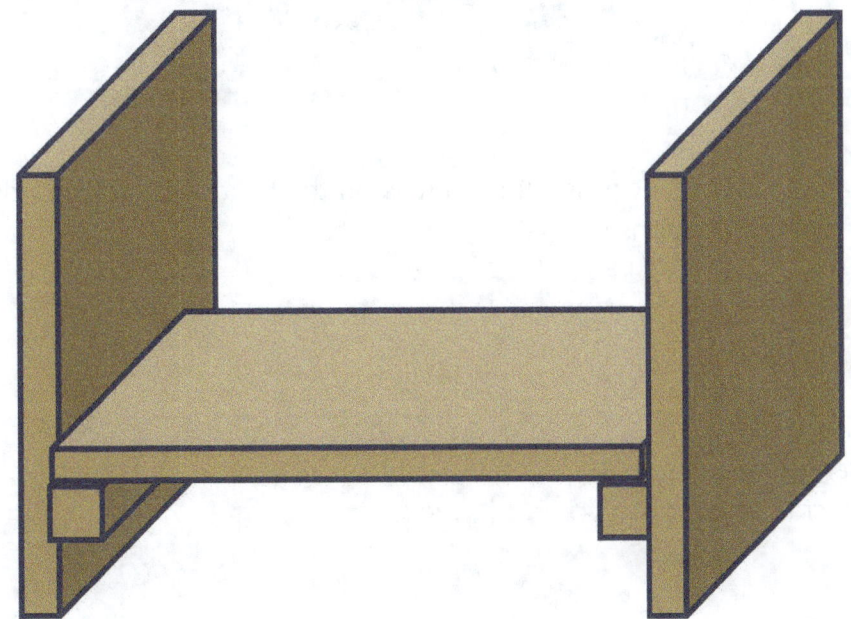

Fancy Double Bed

This bed has a little bit of fanciness with top rails on the head and foot boards. The design offers you fun painting options too.

Materials Needed:

2 - 4" square coasters
2 - ¼ " square dowels cut to 4"
2 - ¼ " x ½" craft wood cut to 4"
Wood glue

Steps:

1. Follow the steps of the Basic Double bed to step 9.
2. Glue the ¼ inch x ½ inch x 4 inch craft board to the top of the headboard and foot board.

3. Hold in place for a few minutes to let the glue start to set.
4. Let glue dry fully, and finish as desired.
5. Let dry fully before you begin playing.

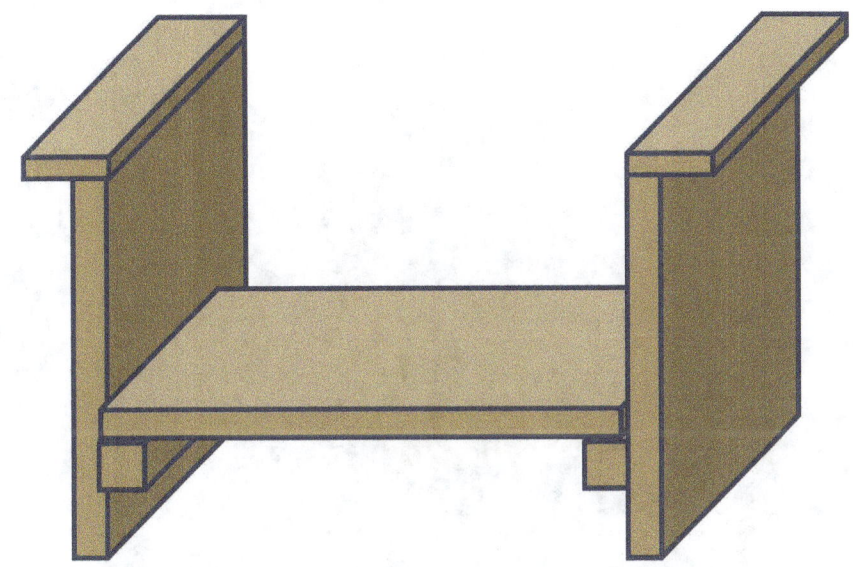

Painting Suggestions

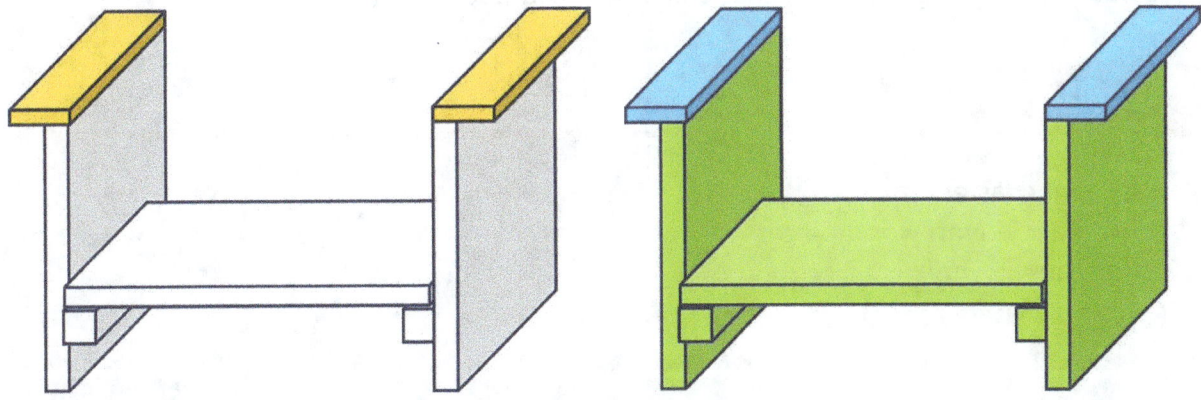

Single Bed

This bed is just the right size for the "children" sized peg dolls (2.5 inch).

Materials Needed

4" square coaster
2 - ¼ x 2 x 3" craft wood pieces
Wood glue
(makes two beds)

Steps

1. Cut the 4" coasters in half.
2. Cut each half in half again. These are the head and foot boards for two beds.
3. Sand your cut edges smooth.
4. Make the bed base by cutting 2 pieces of wood to ¼ inch x 2 inches x 3 inches

5. Measure and mark ½ inch from one edge of each head and foot board.

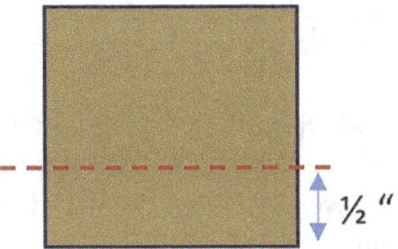

6. Glue the bed base to head and foot boards resting on the ½ inch mark.
7. Hold bed together for a few minutes to let the glue start to set. Proceed once the glue is dry.
8. Apply paint (optional) and let dry fully.
9. Apply clear coat (optional).
10. Let dry fully before you begin playing.

 Did You Make This Project? Share pictures of your creations with our Peg Doll Community. It is a secure platform. Or if you are on Instagram tag #craftedjoypress #pegdollhomes.

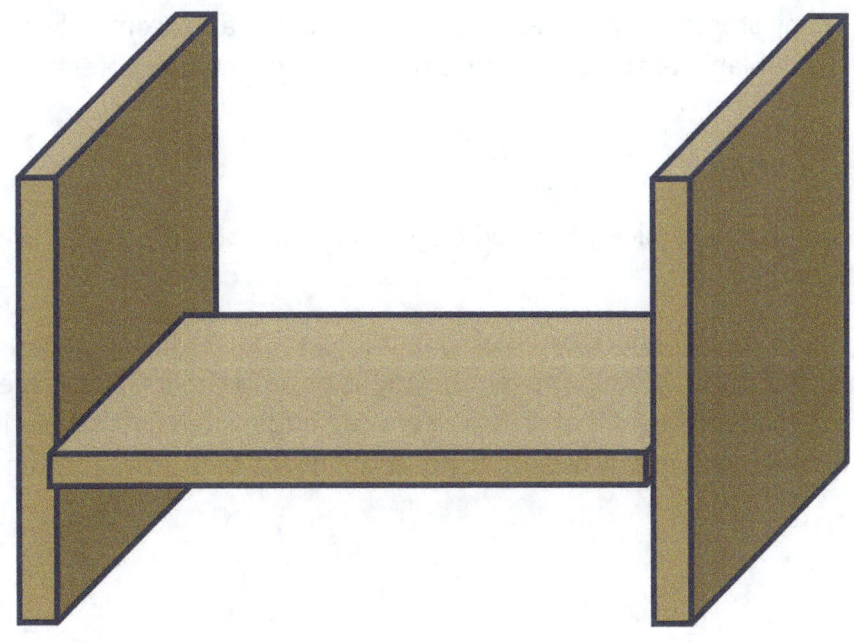

Sewing Bedroom Accessories

Adding bedding is fun. There are several options, such as cut and go, that don't require sewing or use a quick sewing method. Read through these ideas and use the one that works best for you. I have used all of them and I do not have a preference. It really depends on my time and mood.

Cut and Go: No Sewing Required

The simplest way to make bedding is to just cut out a shape and call it good. You can use felt and fabric paint to make wonderful and durable designs. Since this method requires no sewing skills it is simple enough that your child can help. Flannel is also a great option for doll bedding since fleece does not fray and it is very soft, Kids love it! Making items for your dolls is so rewarding especially when your child can help create with you.

Fabric Choice

If you decide to try sewing some accessories, look for fabrics with tighter weaves, such as quilting cotton or tightly woven blends. These fabrics tend to be more durable and less susceptible to fraying, making them ideal for peg doll projects. Flannel is a great option for doll bedding. Many stores sell fat quarters, (material that is approximately 18 x 21 inches). You can get several blankets and doll sleeves out of one of these quarters.

No hemming option

You hem material to have a nicely finished edge, and to keep fabric from fraying. But hemming is not always necessary.

Seam sealants, such as fray check or fabric glue, can be applied to fabric edges to prevent fraying. Another tool that can help prevent fraying is pinking shears. These specialized scissors have zigzag-shaped blades that create a serrated edge when cutting fabric. The zigzag pattern helps minimize fraying by reducing the length of the fabric threads that are exposed.

Stitching

All projects use a basic straight stitch, but feel free to embellish using a zigzag stitch when you are top stitching.

> Tip: Consider upcycling your children's clothing or baby blankets. You can use these no longer needed treasures to create bedding, pillows or rugs for your peg doll play.

● ● ●

Basic No Sew Method

Okay so there really isn't a "method" for no sewing, but more just general consideration concerning fabrics and size.

Fabrics

Felt, flannel and even old fleece blankets (use the less worn parts) make great options for doll blankets. The important aspect of what fabric you choose should be that the fabric is resistant to fraying.

Size

How your child prefers to use the blanket will help determine the size blanket you should make.

Sleep on top play: If you just play with the doll sleeping on top of the blanket, cut the fabric to fit the base of the bed.

- Double bed: 4" x 4"
- Single bed: 2" x 3"

Sleep under play: If you like to place the blanket on top of the doll, cut the fabric about ½ inch wider than the bed base so the blanket will drape over the doll but not smother it.

- Double bed: 4" x 5 ½ - 6"
- Single bed: 3" x 4" – 4 ½ "

At play levels two and three, you may also embellish beds with pillows and bed scarves! Let your child be your guide!

Tip: Want fancier no sew blankets? Use pinking shears on three sides to take it up a notch.

Basic Sewing Method: Double Bed

If you decide to try sewing some accessories, look for fabrics with tighter weaves, such as quilting cotton or tightly woven blends. These fabrics tend to be more durable and less susceptible to fraying, making them ideal for peg doll projects.

Key

 Material - right side

Material – wrong side

– – – – – Sewing line

Seam allowance is ¼"

Step 1

1. Cut your fabric 4 ¾ inches x 9 ½ inches.
2. Place your fabric wrong side up, and fold top and bottom over ¾ inch. Stitch across to attach.

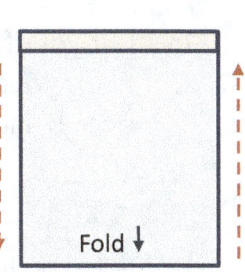

Step 2

1. Fold stitched sides together.
2. Sew the three sides together with a ¼ inch seam allowance.
3. Pink the seams if desired.

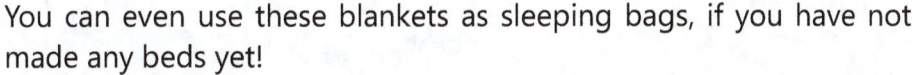

Time to finish up the doll blanket. Your child might like to help with this last step!

You can even use these blankets as sleeping bags, if you have not made any beds yet!

Step 3

1. Fold right side out.
2. Add to doll bed!

• • •

Basic Sewing Method: Single Bed

Sewing the single bed bedding is the same process as the double bed. You are just working with a smaller amount of material!

Key

☐ Material - right side

☐ Material – wrong side

– – – – Sewing line

Seam allowance is ¼"

Step 1

1. Cut your fabric 4 ¾ inches x 9 ½ inches.
2. Place your fabric wrong side up, and fold top and bottom over ¾ inch. Stitch across to attach

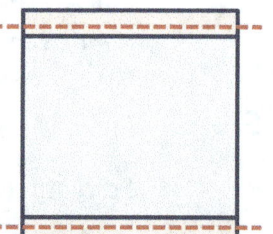

Step 2

1. Fold stitched sides together.
2. Sew the three sides together with a ¼ inch seam allowance.
3. Pink the seams if desired.

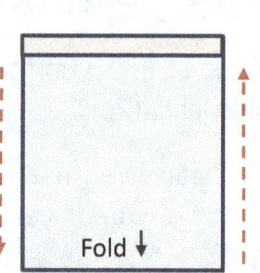

Step 3

1. Fold right side out.
2. Add to doll bed!

Tip: Promoting story telling and reading by reading books or telling stories to your peg doll children!

Basic Sewing Method: No Build Bed Mattress and Bedding

If your dolls need a cushy night's sleep, you can add a mattress to your 3 inch simple plaque bed.

Mattress for 3" wood unfinished plaque bed:

½ " thick high density foam sheet
Materials needed for bedding:
Cotton, flannel or felt fabrics
Mattress cover: 10 ½" x 3 ¼"
Blanket: 3" x 4"

Step 1

Cut your fabric 3 inches x 4 inches using pinking shears to create a decorative and fray resistance edge.

Tip: Use 3mm or 5 mm craft foam sheets for another no sew mattress option.

Envelope Mattress Cover for 3" wood unfinished plaque

Key

Material - right side

Material – wrong side

– – – – – Sewing line

Seam allowance is ¼"

Step 1

1. Cut your fabric 10 ½ inches x 3 ¼ inches.
2. Along the short side of the fabric, fold over ¼ inch and sew an 1/8 " seam across at each end of the fabric.

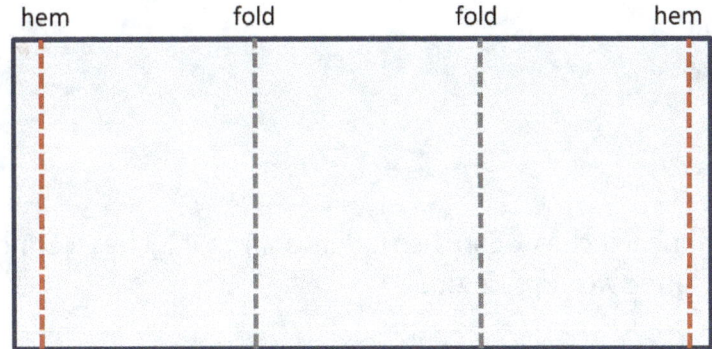

Step 2

1. Place your fabric right side up.
2. Fold stitched sides together toward the middle with about 3/4 inch overlap.

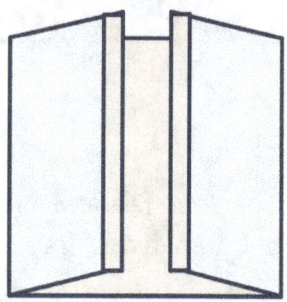

Step 3

1. Sew the two sides together with a ¼ inch seam allowance.
2. Pink the seams if desired.
3. Turn the mattress case right side out.
4. Slip the mattress foam into place.

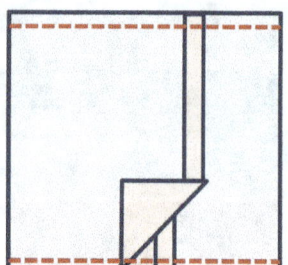

• • •

Doll Sleeve

A doll sleeve is multifunctional, it will protect a doll from chips and scratches when stored or during travel. It also may act as a sleeping bag and bedding. This project is designed to cover the whole doll but you could always make them shorter of you want them to be a sleeping bag with the dolls head poking out.

Key

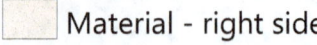 Material - right side

Material – wrong side

– – – – – Sewing line

Seam allowance is ¼"

Step 1

1. Cut your fabric 6 inches x 5 inches (adult doll) or 4 inches x 5 inches (child doll)
2. Place your fabric wrong side up.

3. Along the long side of the adult fabric, fold over ¼ inch and sew an 1/8 inch seam across to the top.
4. For the child doll fabric, since it is square, it does not really matter which edge you choose to fold over for the sleeve opening seam.

Step 2

1. Fold in half with right sides together. Fold on the left.
2. Sew the bottom and right sides together with a ¼ inch seam allowance.

Step 3

1. Turn right side out.
2. Slip in a doll.

Finished Sizes:

Adult: 3" x 4.5"

Child: 1 ½" x 3"

Other Bedroom Accessories: Nightstands

Bedrooms start basic. Just a bed. As your child grows you may add new pieces to the bedroom. A nightstand is a great addition especially if you already have some toy blocks around. Grab a cube and a cylinder (approx. 1 inch x 1 inch) and you are set! We had a roman arch in our block set, and so we used this as a nightstand. If you do not have these smaller blocks already, look for them at resale shops or other places where you can buy gently used toys. Next, we will cover how to make a nightstand with wood craft pieces glued together.

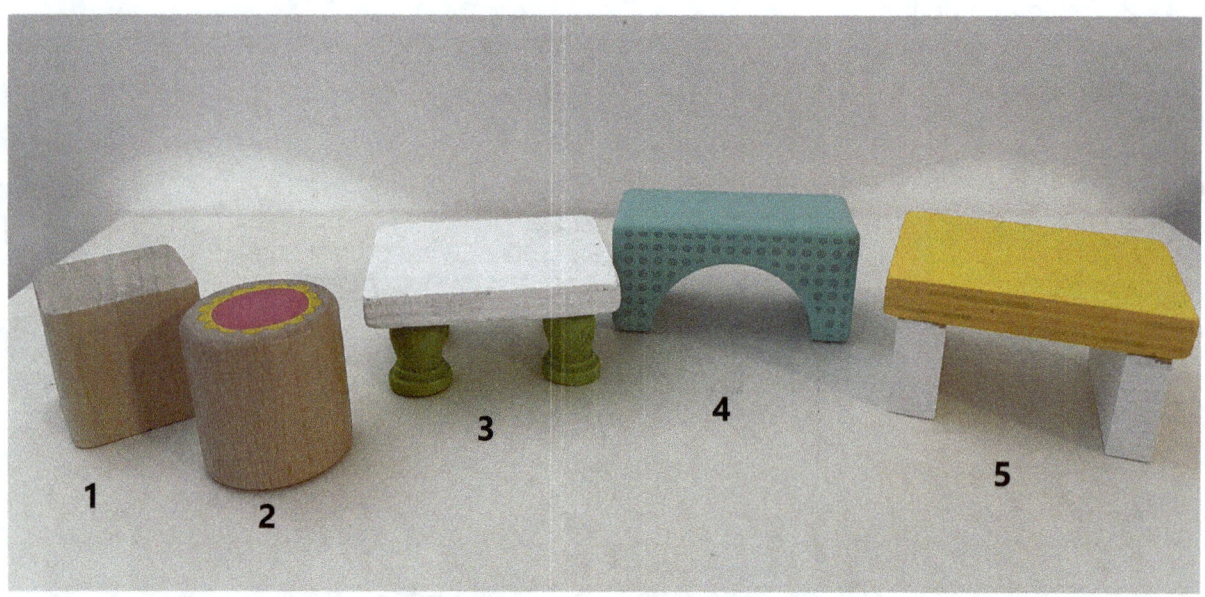

1.   1" cube block.
2.   1" cylinder block.
3.   Wood craft pieces glued together.
4.   Roman arch block.
5.   Cut wood scraps glued together.

Build a Nightstand

As your child's play gets more complex you can make your own nightstands that are a little larger with various wood pieces from the wood craft aisle or cut some scraps to size. We created larger nightstands to have room to add things like a lamp, book and radio.

Materials Needed:

1 ¾ x 2 ¼ x ¼" precut rectangle
4 dowel caps
Wood glue

Steps

1. Apply paint to feet and table. Let dry fully.
2. Glue the four dowel caps with the opening side up in each corner and let dry.
3. Apply clear coat. Let dry fully before playing with.

Tip: Place the feet inset a bit at each corner and evenly spaced for a stable table

Build a Nightstand with solid legs

Materials Needed:

1 ¾ x 2 ¼ x ¼" precut rectangle for tabletop
1 x 1 ¾ x ¼ " wood rectangles for the legs – need 2 (I had some coaster cut offs left over from making a bed that were a good size.)
Wood glue

Steps

1. Sand your wood smooth.
2. Wipe surface with dry cloth to clean.
3. Glue two 1 inch x 1 ¾ inch x ¼ inch scrap wood pieces to the rectangle along each 1 ¾ inch side to be the table legs. Let dry.
4. Apply paint. Let dry fully.
5. Apply clear coat.
6. Let dry fully before play.

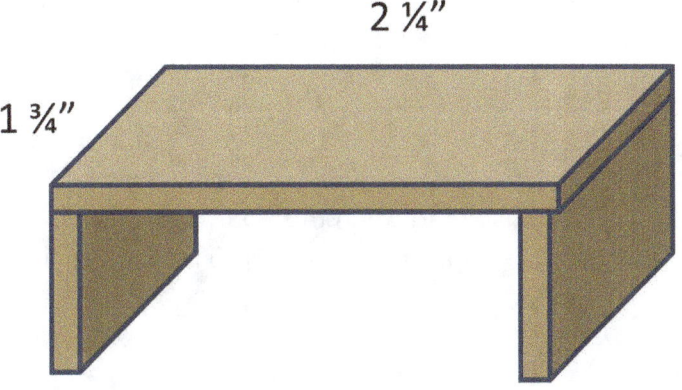

· · ·

Lamps

Table lamps can create a cozy and inviting atmosphere in any room. A bedside reading light is very common in homes, and you can add one to your peg doll home as well. I found unfinished table lamps in a few doll house accessories kits, but I also was able to make some

DIY versions with a few simple shapes. You can even use mushroom shapes to achieve the perfect ambiance.

Make your Own Lamp

Lamps are fun. Place a mini apple shape on top of a dowel cap and viola, a lamp. With some imagination and creativity, you can also create your own unique decor. You can go with a simple painting scheme or get elaborate and try painting on a pattern. I've included some lamp outlines for you to plan out some designs.

Steps

1. Apply paint to apple shape. Add multiple coats if needed. Let dry fully.
2. Apply paint to dowel end cap. Add multiple coats if needed. Let dry fully.
3. Glue the apple (upside down) to the dowel cap's open end (side with hole). Ensure it's stable and centered. Proceed when the glue is dry.
4. Apply clear coat. Let dry fully.

Planning

Use the following outlines to plan out your lamp design

Books and Book Bin

Literacy and the value of reading and books is important in a young child's life. Reinforce the value and joy of reading by including a book bin for your peg dolls. Encourage your child to make up their own stories and book covers as well.

I found a Miniature Wood Cabinet with Drawers at Hobby Lobby and created a book bin for all my peg doll themes.

I used images of book covers of the favorite books we read together. There are lots of conversations you can have around books. One of the greatest outcomes of storytelling is that it inspires children to create their own stories. Create your own book covers that match to stories you like to tell each other.

Tip: Check the copyrights for any image you find on the internet. Look to see if the image is free to use for personal or educational purposes before you use it.

Books

1″ wood square for book

Example of a book cover

Materials Needed:

1″ Wood Squares
Decoupage print outs
Decoupage supplies: brush, decoupage

Decoupage Steps:

1. Cut out your print so it is just slightly smaller than your wood square.
2. Apply a thin layer of decoupage medium to the back of the print.
3. Place your print on the square centering it as much as possible.
4. Apply a thin layer of decoupage medium to the top of the print. And gently smooth it is place.
5. Let decoupage dry.

Tip: Sometimes a child will start to memorize a story that they enjoy reading over and over again. Encourage your child to retell the story to their dolls. Learning to retell a story is an important skill for building reading comprehension and writing skills in young children. Remember, its okay if they do not retell it perfectly. Its all about the practice, your child will increase their abilities as they grow.

Book Bin

Materials Needed:

Mayberry Street Miniatures Miniature Wood Cabinet with Drawers

Book Bin Steps

1. Remove drawers from Miniature Wood Cabinet
2. Optional: Cut off cabinet backsplash.
3. Apply paint to cabinet. Add multiple coats if needed. Let dry fully.
4. Apply clear coat.

Tip: Save the drawers, I used them for other projects in my other books themes. Be sure to check them out! I totally believe in upcycling.

A Cozy Kitchen

Play level guide for building and expanding doll kitchens.

Level 1:

Sink, Stove, Frig, Block table

Level 2:

Sink (from level 1),
Stove (from level 1),
Block table becomes shelf
Add:
Table with knobs feet,
Kitchen accessories/play food

Level 3:

Sink (from level 1),
Toilet (from level 1),
Table (from level 2),
Kitchen accessories (from level 2)
Add:
microwave

Sink and Stove

Cooking, washing hands and doing dishes are all important things for your peg dolls to do, so be sure to include a sink and stove when you begin to create your child's kitchen play set.

Materials Needed:

2" square block See Resource List for where to buy unfinished 2" square blocks
Painting supplies:
Paint of choice
Brush, Water to clean brush
Black permanent marker

Steps:

1. Sand your wood smooth.
2. Wipe surface with dry cloth to clean.
3. Apply paint. Add multiple coats if needed. Let dry fully.
4. Use black permanent marker to draw lines. Let dry fully.
5. Apply clear coat. Let dry fully.

Painting Ideas:

Kitchen Sink

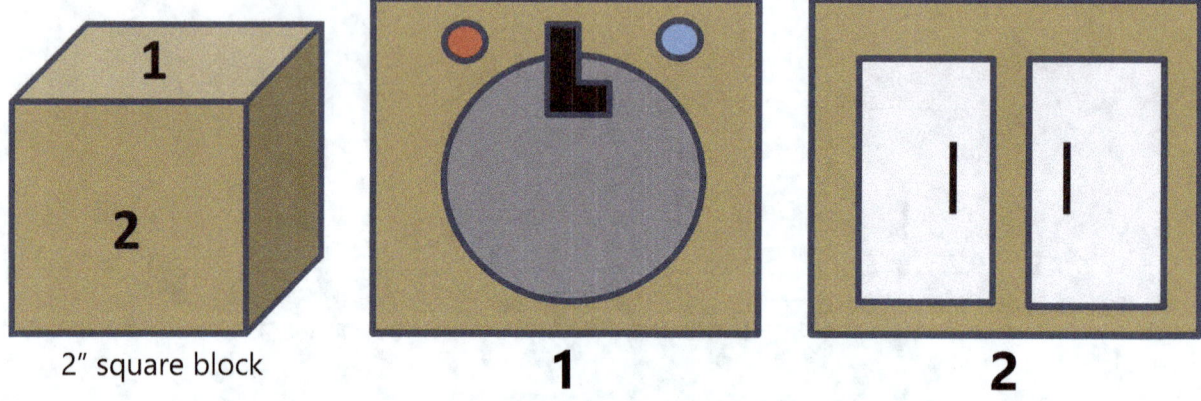

2" square block   1   2

Kitchen Stove

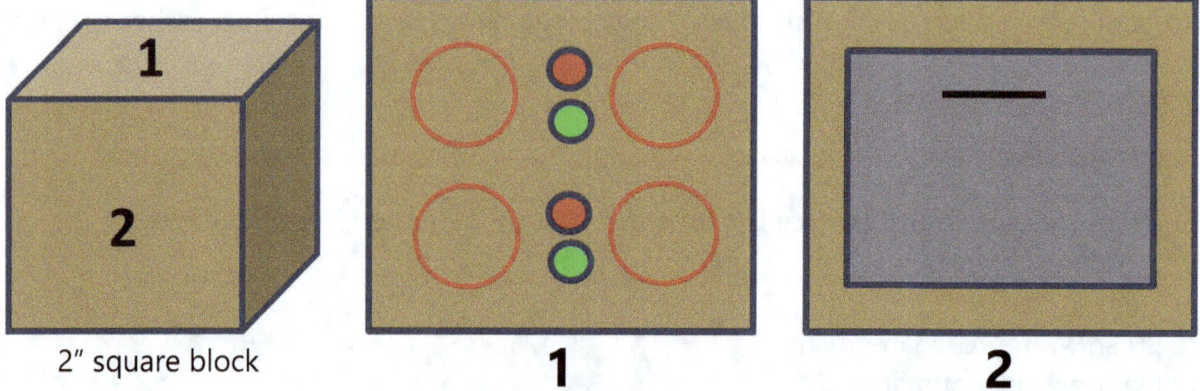

2" square block   1   2

Fridge

Of course, you need a refrigerator, but from my experience, the interest in playing with one comes at the level two stage. As a child grows, their play becomes more involved, then they are interested in having all the kitchen appliances in their play. Use your child's interests as a guide for when to add additional accessories to their playset.

Materials Needed:

1X4 piece of wood
Paint of choice (white, silver, light blue or green)
Painting supplies: Brush, Water to clean brush
Black permanent marker

Steps

1. Cut your wood into a 2 ¼ " X 3 ¾ " rectangular block.

2. Sand your wood smooth.
3. Wipe the surface with dry cloth to clean.
4. Apply paint. Add multiple coats if needed. Let dry fully.
5. Use black permanent marker to draw lines. Use a thin piece of cardboard as a straight edge if desired. Let dry fully.
6. Apply clear coat. Let dry fully.

Painting Ideas:

Decoupage Ideas:

Personalize your peg doll fridge, with photos, child art and / or a grocery list.

Decoupage is quick and easy. I insert and size my images in a word doc program or slides program and print them out. My granddaughters love to see their photos and artwork on the doll fridges. There are lots of fun free clip art online to choose from too!

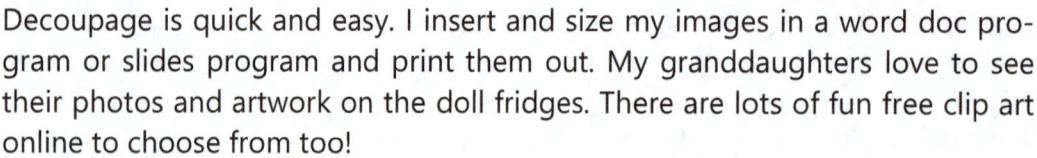

Decoupage prints
Decoupage supplies: Decoupage medium, brush

Steps

1. Apply a thin layer of decoupage medium to the back of the print.
2. Place your print on the fridge where you want it to be.
3. Apply a thin layer of decoupage medium to the top of the print. And gently smooth it is place.
4. Let the decoupage dry.

Patterns – decoupage actual size

Table

A rectangular block is very easy to imagine as a table and easy to make as well. Start off making this simple table. As your child's play progresses you can substitute it out for a fancier table and turn this block on its side to become a counter or shelf later.

Materials Needed:

2"X 4" Wood
Painting supplies: paint, brush, water to clean brush

Steps

1. Cut a 2" x 4" wood block to be 3 ¼" long.
2. Sand all edges to be a little rounded and smooth. You can also use a handheld router on the edges if you have one.
3. Paint and finish as you desire.

Fancy Table

I found these great wooden "tables" at Hobby Lobby on sale. Throughout the year you can find them in seasonal colors, so once they are 50% off, they cost about the same as making your own. I think they are time consuming to repaint so if I cannot find them in the color, I want I simply buy an unfinished wood plaque and ball knobs and quickly make my own so I can paint them my preferred color.

Materials Needed:

3" wood unfinished plaque
1" ball knobs for table legs (need 3)
Wood glue
Painting supplies: paint, brush, water to clean brush

I personally like using ball knobs as table feet. They are very stable and make the table the right height.

You can always check out other wood turnings to use as table legs. The 1" candle cups are also cute and sturdy as table legs.

Steps

1. Sand your wood smooth.
2. Wipe the surface with dry cloth to clean.
3. Glue the 3 ball knob legs on following the pattern for the circle. Rectangle or square forms should have 4 legs glued in each corner.
4. Apply paint. Add multiple coats if needed. Let dry fully.
5. Apply clear coat. Let dry fully.

Fancy Table Assembly

Space the knobs in an equal triangle.

Set the knobs so they are even with the table edge or inset just slightly.

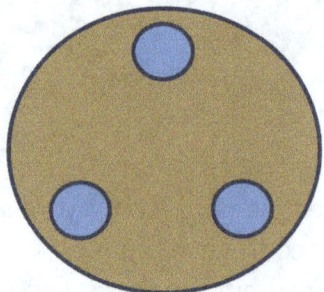

Other Ideas

Of course the table does not need to be round. You can try a 3–4-inch square or rectangular plaque as well. Just remember these will need four feet.

Microwave

Microwaves are a common kitchen appliance. If your child is interested in adding a microwave to their kitchen it is very easy to make.

Materials Needed:

1 ¼' h x 1 ½' w block of wood
Painting supplies: paint, brush, water to clean brush
Black permanent marker

Steps

1. Cut block of wood to size.
2. Sand all edges to be a little rounded and smooth.
3. Apply base coat of paint.

4. Paint details. I like to place a piece of painter's tape in the center of the block and draw around it with a Sharpie to get straight lines.
5. Apply clear coat. Let dry fully.

Painting Ideas:

 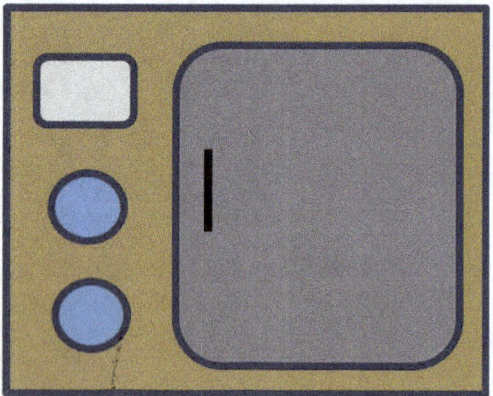

Miniature Cups, Plates and Food

Miniatures require fine motor skills, and these small accessories are great at helping children develop dexterity and imagination.

These are some examples of kitchen accessories you may want to add to your play set. I like to keep the wood aesthetic, and I do not buy doll house miniatures that are decorations and have the warning that they are not toys.

Another advantage to wooden kitchen accessories is that they can be left unpainted or painted to suggest an item such as a cupcake or pie. You can also paint plates and cups to match any décor.

Note: See Resource List for where to buy kitchen accessories.

DIY Kitchen Accessories

3

Materials Needed:

Checkers = plates
Small button plugs = cupcakes
Large button plugs = pie
Wooden nickels = pizza
Dowel caps = cups
Mini apples – you can buy at Woodpeckers crafts

Steps

1. Apply base coat of paint.
2. Paint details. I like to use dots of paint. I do use a Sharpie on the cupcakes to add sprinkles, but I wait to ensure the sharpie lines are set. Sharpies tend to smear when you apply the clear coat too soon.
3. Apply clear coat. Let dry fully.

Painting Ideas:

   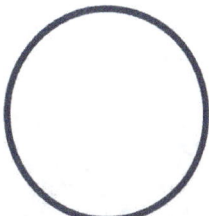 

Circles for Pizza, Pancakes etc.

Rectangles for Flat Breads, Casseroles, Waffles

1 ¼ inch furniture plugs and larger for cupcake, pie and cake painting ideas and planning space:

   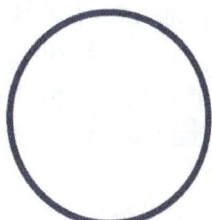 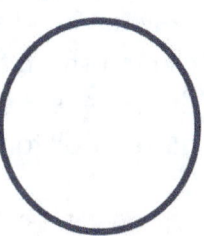

Kitchen Shelf

Where are you going to put all your kitchen accessories, your mason jars, cupcakes and pies? Why not build a simple shelf? Shelf frames or wood "boxes" are easy to find at craft stores. I can transform the box by sanding it and repainting it. I find good sized unfinished boxes at the dollar store that don't require any extra prep, and the price makes it very affordable to make. Look for boxes that are at least an inch deep so they will be stable when played with.

Materials Needed:

Wood box frame
Craft wood that is the same width as the box to cut to size to be shelves.
Painting supplies: paint, brush, water to clean brush

Steps

1. Prepare your wood box frame if needed.
2. Cut your craft wood shelves to size.

3. Sand the cut edges smooth.
4. Glue shelves in place. Use spacer blocks to keep your shelves level and even when glueing them in
5. Apply clear coat. Let dry fully.

Tip: If you would like a stained wood finish, water down your paint to create a stain

Bathroom

Play level guide for building and expanding doll bathrooms

 1    2    3

Level 1:

Sink,
Basic tub,
Toilet

Level 2:

Sink (from level 1),
Toilet (from level 1)
Add:
Tub with knobs
and/or faucet

Level 3:

Sink (from level 1)
Toilet (from level 1)
Tub with knobs (from level 2)
Add:
Child stool
Shower

Bathroom Sink

Wash your face and brush your teeth before bedtime. Every peg doll should develop good hygiene habits, so create a bathroom sink to help facilitate learning and play. The sink is a basic project that only requires painting a block to resemble a sink.

Materials Needed:

2" square block
Painting supplies: paint, brush, water to clean brush
Black permanent marker

Steps

1. Sand your wood smooth.
2. Wipe surface with dry cloth to clean.
3. Apply paint. Add multiple coats if needed. Let dry fully.
4. Use black permanent marker to draw lines. Let dry fully.
5. Apply clear coat. Let dry fully.

Painting Suggestion

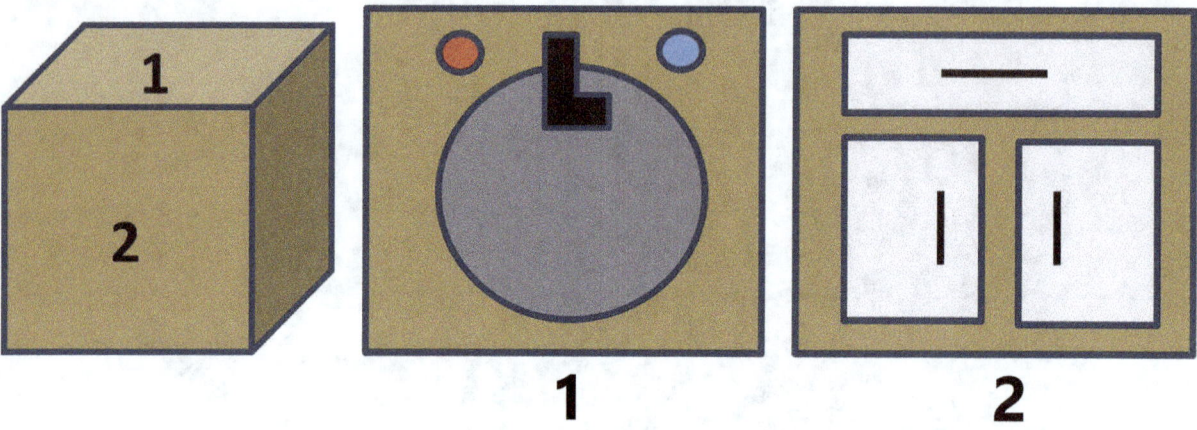

1   2

Tip: I like to paint the bathroom sink differently than the kitchen sink to distinguish to myself the different room sets. When we play it doesn't matter what sink is used in a room.

Bathroom Tub

Bathtime is fun. Creating a tub is also very simple. You just need to decide how you want to paint it. You can just paint the inside, paint the whole tub or even embellish the tub sides to look like tile. I went with simple, quick and easy.

Materials Needed:

3″ wood unfinished plaque
Painting supplies: paint, brush, water to clean brush

Steps

1. Sand your wood smooth.
2. Wipe surface with dry cloth to clean.
3. Apply paint. Add multiple coats if needed. Let dry fully.
4. Apply clear coat. Let dry fully.

Tip: See Sewing Bathroom Accessories for instructions on how to make a simple towel.

Fancy Bathroom Tub

Rub a dub dub who wants a fancier tub? One day my granddaughter wanted to know where the hot water was. Hmmm good question, well let's just add some knobs to our tub then.

Materials Needed:

3" wood unfinished plaque
¼" axle dowel caps (need 2)
¼" dowel cut ¾" long
¼" dowel cut ¾" long
1/8" dowel cut ¾" long
Wood glue
Painting supplies: paint, brush, water to clean brush

Steps

1. Cut the dowels to size.
2. Drill a shallow 1/8" hole (approx. 1/8" deep) in the side of the ¼"dowel.
3. Glue the 1/8" dowel into the hole to be the tub spout. Allow it to dry.

4. Paint the interior of plaque if you are creating a new tub from scratch.
5. Glue the spout unit to the center of the short end of the tub base, and the ¼" axle dowel caps on either side to be the tub knobs.
6. Apply a dot of paint to the top of each knob to indicate hot and cold water.
7. Apply clear coat. Let dry fully.

• • •

Other Bathroom Tub Ideas

I found a round wooden trinket tray in the sale section at a store. I sanded the quote down in the middle, painted it and it became a spa tub. Keep an eye out for wooden items that can easily be transformed such as this one.

Tip: A bathtub can also be a piece of felt cut in the shape of a rectangle or circle. Remember you do not need to add every accessory all at once. Adding a little at a time keeps the play fresh.

Bathroom Toilet

Toilets are fixtures in our bathrooms and can be added to your peg doll dollhouse play at about level two. Children who are potty training can become aware of their peg dolls who need to use the potty too. What is it that they say? Everybody poops!

Materials Needed:

¼" x 1 ½" x 1 ¾ " wood board
½ " x 1 ½" x 1 ¾ "wood board
¼" Axle Dowel Caps (need 4)
Wood glue
Painting supplies: paint, brush, water to clean brush

Steps

1. Cut wood boards to size.

2. Glue the ¼" thick wood board to the ½" thick board along the 1 ¾" sides of each board. Form an "L" shape. Let dry.

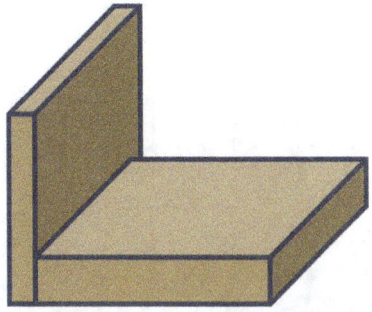

3. Glue the four axle dowel caps to the bottom four corners of the ½" thick board. Let dry.

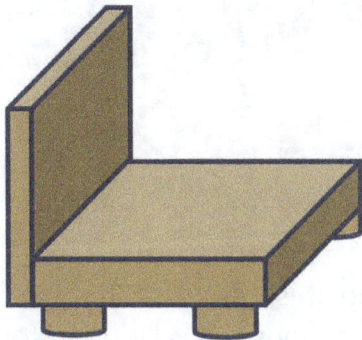

4. Paint as desired.
5. Apply clear coat. Let dry fully.

Painting Suggestion

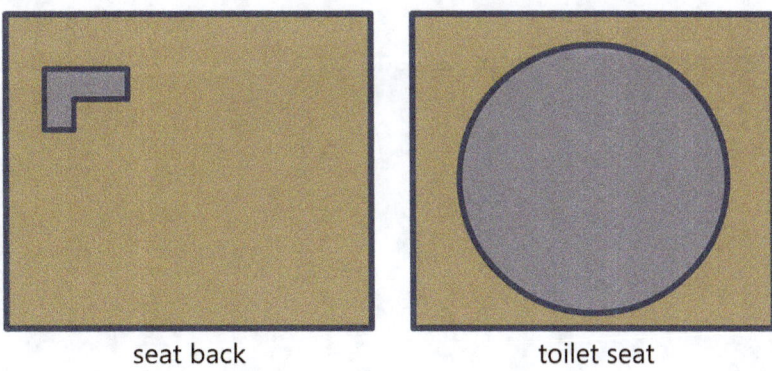

seat back   toilet seat

Bathroom Stool

When your child is potty training, it is fun to add the furniture your child may be using in the bathroom to your peg doll dollhouse play. Using a stool is a sign of growing up, and it just so happens to also help the peg doll child dolls reach the bathroom sink better as well. The stool is a quick and easy project that adds lots of conversational opportunities as well.

Materials Needed:

¼ " x 1" x 1 ½" piece of wood
¼' x 1 ¼" Axle Dowel Caps (need 4)
Painting supplies: paint, brush, water to clean brush

Steps

Note: If you are going to paint the stool all the same color you may start with step 3 and then proceed with the painting and finishing.

1. Apply paint to stool base. Add multiple coats if needed. Let dry.
2. Apply paint to dowel caps if desired.
3. Glue the four axle dowel caps to the four corners of the stool base. They will be touching on the 1″ side of the block. That is okay. Let dry.
4. Apply clear coat. Let dry fully.

Painting Suggestion

 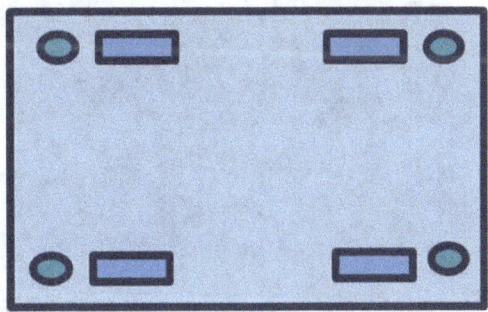

Bathroom Shower

To shower or not to shower. Some children will like their peg dolls to have a shower. If your child is one of those, this shower offers an open design that makes it easy to play with.

Steps

1. Cut the circular coaster in half. This is the shower base.
2. Sand your wood smooth.
3. Apply paint to areas and pieces you wish to paint. Add multiple coats if needed. Let dry fully.

4. Glue shower head and knobs in place on the square coaster. Let dry.
5. Glue the half circle shower base to the square coaster. Let dry.
6. Apply clear coat. Let dry fully.

Shower Assembly

Since you will have another half circular coaster, make a couple of showers. You might paint one and have your child paint the other.

Get creative with this project, use stencils or wasabi tabi tape to decorate the shower! No worries about it actually getting wet!

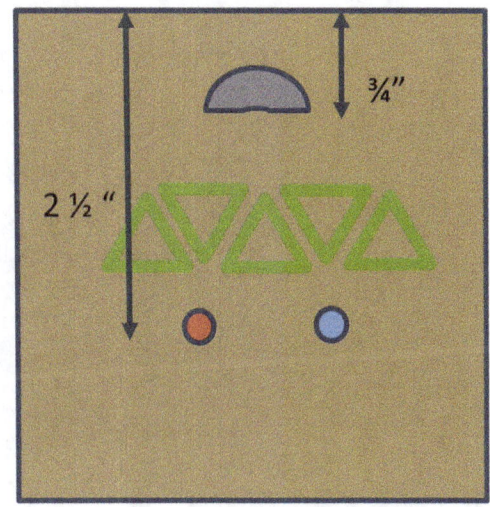

Sewing Bathroom Accessories

Bathroom Towel

Add a bath towel to your bathroom. Of course, this is just a suggested size. Feel free to customize items to your doll set. You can opt for either a no sew method or hem the edges of your towels.

Material Suggestions:

Cotton, felt, fleece
Size:
1 ¼" x 2 ¾"/ 3.5 cm x 7 cm

Steps

Cut material to size with pinking shears to reduce fray or if sewing, allow for a ¼" seam allowance. Since felt isn't prone to fray, pinking edges is a nice decorative effect.

Bathroom Rug

A bath rug can add a nice homey feel to your bathroom. Of course, this is just a suggested size. Feel free to customize items to your doll set. Explore other shapes and sizes.

Material Suggestions:

Cotton, felt sheet
Size: 6 ½ inch diameter / 17 cm diameter

Steps

Cut material to size with pinking shears to reduce fraying.

Even though felt isn't prone to fray, I still use pinking shears to cut out the rug. They add a nice decorative effect to your rugs.

Tip: Use a container lid that is this approximate size and trace around it to get a nice even circle shape

Livingroom

Play level guide for building and expanding doll living rooms.

The living room in peg doll play is often just a sitting room. I introduce some living room furniture at stage two play and then add level three pieces later.

2

3

Level Two Accessories

Couch,
Chair,
Coffee table,
Fireplace

Level Three Accessories

Television,
Vacuum,
Floor Clock,
Floor Lamp,
Radio,
House plants

Couch Bench

A peg doll couch should be pretty low to the ground, so it is stable for dolls to "sit" on. You can introduce a simple bench design first and if the couch is preferred, then build the couch in the next project for your dolls.

Materials Needed:

¼ " x 3 ½ " x 1 ½" piece of wood
Four ¼' x 1 ¼" Axle Dowel Caps
Painting Finish:
Painting supplies: paint, brush, water to clean brush
Decoupage finish:
Material cut to size of the wood 3 ½ " x 1 ½"
Decoupage supplies: brush, decoupage

Steps

1. Cut your wood to size.

2. Sand your wood smooth.
3. Wipe the surface with dry cloth to clean.
4. Finish the bench as desired. You can leave it unpainted or paint. You may also call it done or apply a decoupage finish.

Steps for Decoupage Finish

5. Cut your material to size with pinking shears.
6. Apply decoupage to one side of the wood and place material on top, smooth as needed. Let dry fully.
7. Apply a second coat of decoupage to the top on the material for added durability.
8. Glue four legs in each corner on the wood side without the fabric.

Fancy Couch

This couch is super cute and made with coasters. It looks impressive for being such a simple project.

Materials Needed:

4" solid wood coaster
4 Square Welled Pinewood Coasters
¼' x 1 ¼" Axle Dowel Caps (need 4)
Painting supplies: paint, brush, water to clean brush

Steps

1. Cut the welled coaster 2 ½ inches from one side. Your finished size will be 4 inches wide x 2 ½ inches high. This is the back of the couch.

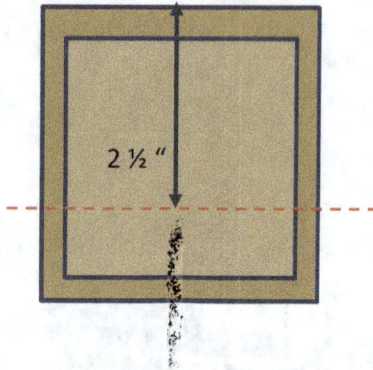

2. From the solid coaster, cut out a piece of wood 1 ¾ inches x 3 ½ inches; this is the seat of the couch. It will slide into the welled part of the couch back.

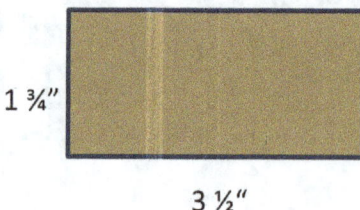

3. Take the other half of the welled coaster (approx. 4 inches wide x 1 ½inches high) and measure 1 ¾ inches from either edge. These will be the couch arms.

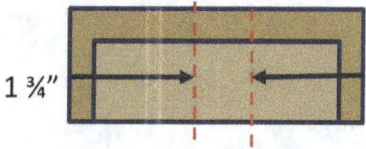

4. Sand all your edges smooth.
5. Glue couch base to couch back (welled coaster) The couch base should fit inside the welled section. Let dry.

6. Glue the couch arms to either side of the couch base with the welled side facing out. Let dry.

7. Turn the couch over and glue axle dowel caps in each corner.
8. Paint and varnish as desired.

Fancy Chair

Next comes the living room chair. You make the chair with basically the same process as the couch, except the back is solid and you only use the welled coaster for the arms. Let's give it a try.

Materials Needed:

4" solid wood coaster
4 Square Welled Pinewood Coasters
¼' x 1 ¼" Axle Dowel Caps (need 4)
Painting supplies: paint, brush, water to clean brush

Steps

1. From the solid coaster, cut out a piece of wood 2 ½ inches wide x 2 ¼ inches high. This is the back of the chair. Optionally, you can sand the top two corners to round them off.
2. From the solid coaster, cut out a piece of wood 1 ½ inches x 1 ¾ inches. This is the seat of the chair.
3. Take the welled coaster and measure a 1 ½ " square from two corners. These will be the chair arms.
4. Sand all your edges smooth.
5. Glue one chair arm (welled side facing out) and glue the chair seat to the chair back. Let dry.
6. Glue the other chair arm on. Let dry.
7. Turn the chair over and glue the axle dowel caps in each corner.

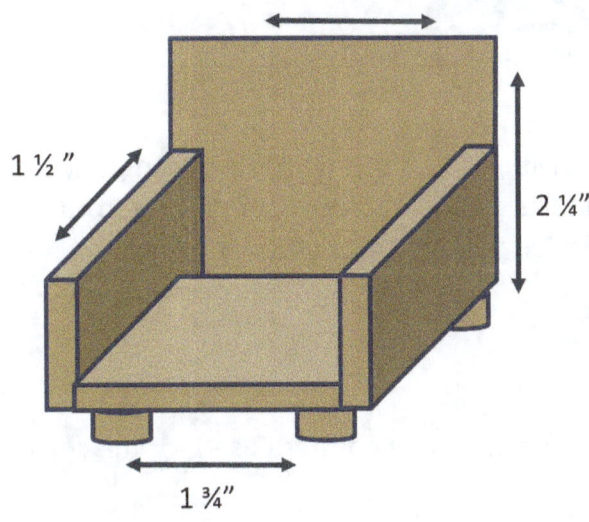

1 ½ "

2 ¼"

1 ¾"

Coffee and Side Table

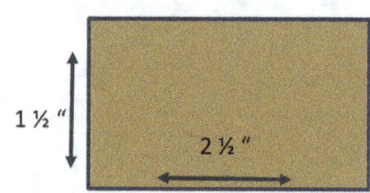

The living room tables add a bit of play interactivity, when they are used for lamps, radios, books etc. Just like with the nightstands, side tables can be 1" blocks or cylinders from your block collection. I have a simple coffee table design you might want to try as well.

Materials Needed:

¼ " x 2 ½ " x 1 ½ "wood (I cut mine from the solid square coaster I used for the chair and couch
¼" to ½" beads (need 4) Or 1 " blocks
Painting supplies: paint, brush, water to clean brush

Steps

1. Cut your wood to size.
2. Sand your wood smooth.
3. Apply paint to table base if desired. Let dry fully.
4. Glue four beads in each corner of the rectangle table base for the legs.
5. Apply clear coat. Let dry fully.

1 ½ "

2 ½ "

Fireplace

Who doesn't love a cozy fire in the fireplace? This project is so simple that it makes it irresistible not to include. All you need is one of those 3 inch wood unfinished plaques, like what you can use to make a bed or a tub. Now it becomes a fireplace! When the wood is unpainted it is slightly rough so the felt flames stick well to the inside.

Materials Needed:

Fireplace: 3" wood unfinished plaque
Logs: ¼" dowel cut 2 ½ " long
¼" dowel cut 1 ¾ " long
¼" dowel cut 1" long
Fire Flames: Red or orange felt

Steps for a Painted Fireplace

1. Apply base paint or stain to entire plaque. Stain is just watered down paint. If you use stain, test it on a piece of scrap wood to make sure you get the exact color you want. Let dry fully.

2. Paint the fireplace background by sponging on a little black and dark gray paint. Let dry fully.
3. Paint fire flames.
4. Apply clear coat. Let dry fully.

Steps for Logs

1. If you are using dowels cut the dowels to size.
2. Paint or stain them to your preferred color.
3. Glue the dowels together to make a pyramid. They are easier to play with as one piece.
4. Apply clear coat. Let dry fully.

Tip: You can also cut up some dry twigs that are the right diameter. Remove the bark. Do not use "green" wood.

Steps for Flame

1. Use the pattern on the right as a suggested size for a basic flame.
2. Cut it out.
3. Since the inside of the plaque is a little rough, the flame should stick but will be removable.

Tip: I prefer to create more interactive toys so you and your child can actually build the fire. Another option though is to glue the flame on the fireplace and build the fire by adding the logs.

Television

To add a screen or not, is something I waited on until my grandchildren asked for one. You can create one of any size, super large big screen style or small for a suggestion of a screen that could be a TV or computer. See the microwave pattern (1 ¼ inch x 1 ½ inch block of wood). This pattern is for a medium floor style television.

Materials Needed:

2 x 2 x ¼ " wood square
¼ " square dowel
Painter's tape
Wood glue
Painting supplies: paint, brush, water to clean brush

Steps

1. Sand your wood smooth.
2. Wipe surface with dry cloth to clean.
3. Tape ¼ inch border around wood square and paint center black, silver or light blue. Let dry fully.
4. Paint base wood dowel color of your choice.
5. Glue TV square wood to base. Let dry.
6. Apply clear coat. Let dry fully.

Interactive Television

I had a wooden center mount drawer slide from an old dresser remodel project. I have found so many uses for this piece of wood. In this project, you create a TV base out of the drawer slide and then you can have several "TV pieces of wood" to slide into the slot to make the TV interactive. You can decoupage specific shows on your TV wood squares.

Materials Needed:

2" x 2" x ¼ " wood squares (as many as you need)
Wood center mount drawer slide 2 ½" long
Painting supplies: Brush, Water to clean brush, varnish
Decoupage prints to suggest TV shows, go with generic images for more open-ended play
Decoupage supplies: brush, decoupage

Steps

1. Cut the center mount drawer slide to size.
2. Sand edges smooth
3. Paint if desired.
4. Decoupage your TV show prints onto the 2 inch x 2 inch wood squares. You can use one or both sides.

 **Tip:** I prefer to use generic images instead of images from actual TV shows. You can be more creative in making up stories about what your dolls are watching on the TV

• • •

Long Clock or Floor Clock

Hickory Dickory Dock, yes, we needed a clock .... and a mouse. This was one of those special times when my granddaughter was interested in a fun rhyme, and I created the props for our peg doll play. It also goes very nicely in a living room.

Materials Needed:

Wood block ¾" x 1 ¾" x 5"
1 ¼" craft wood circle
Painting Supplies: brushes and paint
Clock face print out
Decoupage supplies: brush, decoupage

Steps

1. Cut a 1 inch x4 inch piece of wood to size. This is the clock body.
2. Sand one end into a semi circle. Router or sand the edges.
3. Decoupage the clock face onto the craft circle.
4. Paint clock details as shown in the picture.
5. Glue clock face circle to clock body on the curved end of the clock.
6. Set the time on the clock.
7. Apply clear coat. Let dry fully.

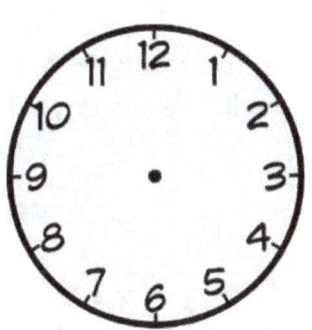

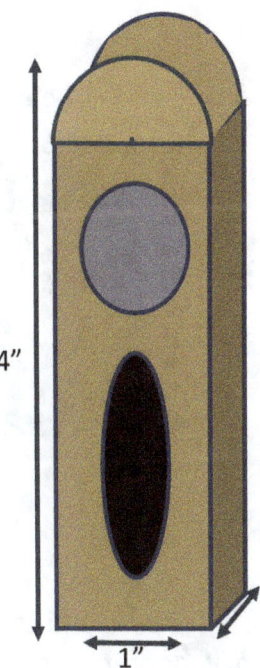

4"

1"

Radio

A cute accessory to add to your basic doll play is a radio. The radio is fun to move from room to room and can get your dolls singing and dancing! Call it what makes sense for your family, boombox, speakers.... It is a great prop to get everyone singing and dancing.

Materials Needed:

¾"d x ¾" h x 1 ¼" h wood block
½" wood craft circle
Craft toothpick dowel cut ¾" long

Steps

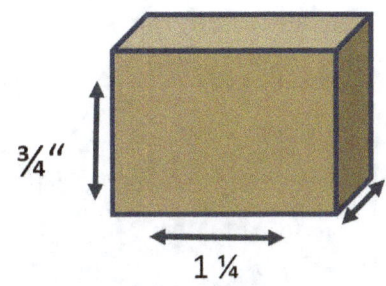

1. Cut your wood block to size.
2. Sand your wood smooth.
3. Use a 3/32 drill bit to drill a hole for antenna approx. ¼" deep off to one side of the block.
4. Paint block, circle and antennae dowel as desired. Let dry fully.
5. Glue circle and antennae on following the pattern shown.
6. Paint knob details on radio if desired
7. Apply clear coat. Let dry fully.

Painting Suggestion

 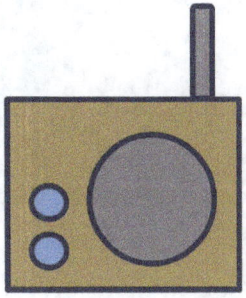

Floor Lamp

Floor lamps can be used in a variety of ways to create different looks or create style in a room. Children like to experiment with styles through their play as much as adults. Although they might not be aware of it, that is exactly what they do as they plan out and arrange their doll's rooms. Add a few different floor lamp styles for your child to play with. This is the basic lamp pattern, and the fancy lamp is on the next page.

Materials Needed:

1" wood wheel
1" flower pot
½" bead with ¼ " hole
¼ " dowel cut 4 ¼ " long

Steps

1. Cut your ¼ inch dowel to size.
2. Glue dowel into wood wheel. This is the lamp base.
3. Place your ½ inch bead on the dowel. This will help you keep the flowerpot shade in position while you are glueing it.
4. Put the flowerpot on the bead and arrange the bead / pot combo so the flowerpot is at the top of the dowel.
5. Glue the flowerpot in place.

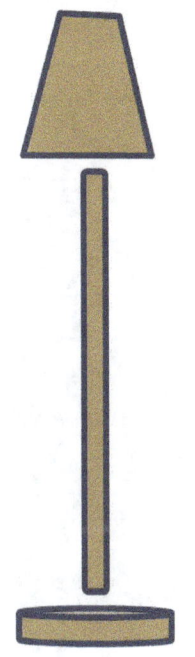

Floor lamps can be so much fun to make. Get your creative juices flowing by coming up with different embellishments such as adding beads or using different sizes of dowels and shades to give your lamp some individual style.

Embellishment Ideas

1. Add a bead on top of the base and a "pull chain" with a string and smaller bead. Simply glue these items in place.
2. The basic lamp style.
3. A fancy arch floor lamp. See following section.
4. Lamp with a bead base, larger dowel and larger flowerpot shade.

Fancy Floor Lamp

I have always liked the elegance of an arched floor lamp. I gave myself the challenge of trying to make one that would be simple enough to recreate. Hope you like it.

Materials Needed:

1 ½ " wood wheel
1" flowerpot
¾ " bead with ¼ " hole (need two)
¼ " dowel cut 4 ½ "long
1" wood ring

Steps

1. Cut your ¼ inch dowel to size.
2. Cut your 1 inch ring in half
3. Glue dowel into wood wheel. This is lamp base.
4. Place a bead on the dowel at the base and on the top.
5. Glue one end of the half ring into the bead at the top of the lamp and glue the other end into the flowerpot shade.
6. Gently hold pieces in place until the glue has set.
7. Let dry fully before playing.

• • •

Vacuum

Cleaning is just a fact of life. So your peg dolls may want a vacuum to make housework fun.

Materials Needed:

1x4 wood block cut to ¾ " x1 " x 1 ½"
½" x 1" rectangle craft wood.
Wood Tie Rack Peg

Steps

1. Cut your wood block to size.
2. Sand your wood smooth.
3. Cut your rectangle of craft wood to size. Since this wood is so thin you can also just snap off the part you do not want.
4. Drill a hole for the vacuum handle. I created a jig to help get the angle right.
5. Paint the vacuum base and the rectangle craft wood. Let dry.
6. Glue the rectangle of craft wood to the front of the vacuum.
7. Paint the wood tie rack peg.
8. Glue the peg into the vacuum base.
9. Apply clear coat. Let dry fully.

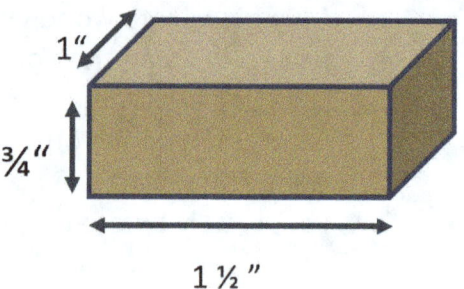

Painting Suggestion

House Plants

Greenery adds so much to our homes. A good way to build appreciation for plants is to add it to your child's play. They will see firsthand how a simple plant will add something special to a room. I have two options for you. Make the plants out of wood for an all-wood option or use plastic mini succulents and candle cups for pots.

Materials Needed:

¼" x 1 ½" x wood
Painting supplies: paint, brush, water to clean brush
Permanent marker for details

Steps

1. Trace one of the plant shapes onto your wood.
2. Cut out the plant shapes with a coping or band saw.
3. Sand your wood smooth.
4. Wipe the surface with dry cloth to clean.
5. Apply paint to all pieces. Add multiple coats if needed. Let dry fully.
6. Apply clear coat and let dry fully.

Plant Shape Suggestions

Use the following shapes as guides.

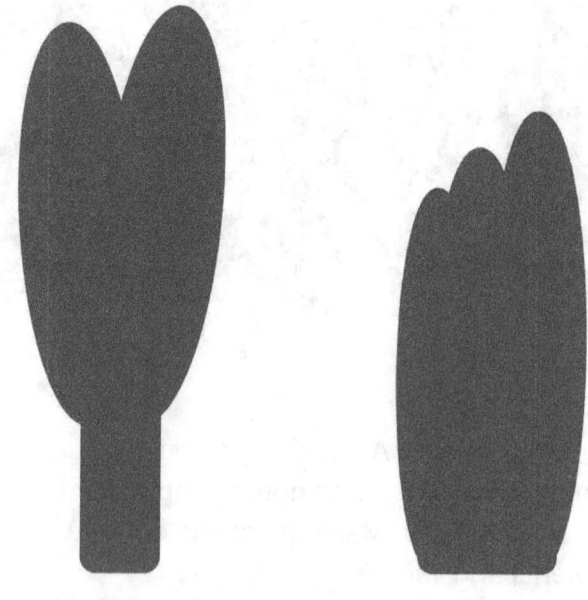

Interactive House Plants

Buying plastic succulent plants is a fun option. What makes this so fun is when you and your child can assemble the plants. Buy a few different styles for variety.

Materials Needed:

Various mini succulents
Large candle cup: 1.38" x 1.38" x 1.57"

Steps

Snip the end off the faux plant with wire cutters. Ensure there is no exposed wire at the end for safe playing. Seal the end with electrical tape.

Sewing Living Room Accessories

Living Room Rugs

Rugs are fun to decorate with. If you choose not to paint your living room furniture, they will add a pop of color to your play. The size of your rug will depend on your playscape and should be customizable to your taste. If you use a 10x10 wood frame to play on, a 6" circle will fit well.

Materials Suggestions:

cotton, felt sheet
Size:
6 ½ inch diameter / 17 cm diameter

Steps

1. Cut material to size
2. Finish the edges with pinking shears to reduce fray.

Even though felt isn't prone to fray, I still use pinking shears to cut out the rug. They add a nice decorative effect to your rugs.

Tip: Use a container lid that is this approximate size and trace around it to get a nice even circle shape.

Couch Pillows

3

Pillows are quick and easy. Since you are working with a small piece of material, I don't sweat the finished product too much. I use cotton for pillows instead of felt because I think it is easier to work with.

Materials Suggestions:

Cotton, flannel
batting material or scrap cloth
Size:
1 ¼" x 2 ½ "

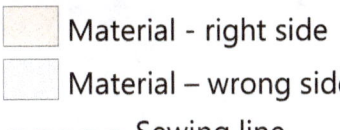
Material - right side

Material – wrong side

– – – – – Sewing line

Seam allowance is ¼"

Steps

1. Cut material to size with pinking shears to reduce fraying.
2. Fold in half with right sides together.
3. Sew a ¼ inch seam allowance along three sides.

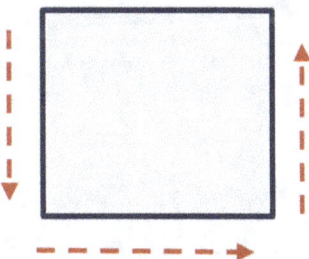

4. Turn right side out.
5. Stuff with batting Do not over fill.
6. Fold exposed seams in and top stitch the fourth side closed.

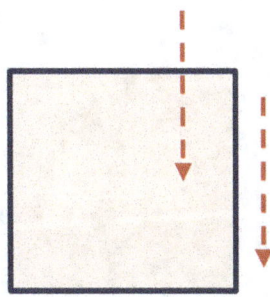

Play Environments

Every magical tale needs a place to come alive.

Although multilevel doll houses have been around for a very long time, I often find children play on the floor outside the doll house. Also doll houses are not that mobile if a child wants to play with their dolls in another room. A child cannot independently bring the dollhouse outside or to another room without help. Using simple wooden frames eliminates all of these complications. These simple wood bases give the framework for rooms, they are easy to arrange and allow more creativity because the child can imagine the base as a room as part of a house or as a stand-alone destination such as a store.

The larger bases can be a multi roomed unit (kitchen and family room) and the smaller bases placed around it to create a multi roomed home (bedrooms, bathroom, playroom). The wooden bases are also easier to store, reducing clutter in a child's room. They are easy for the child to set up their play indoors or out, travel with one or generally just be more versatile and empowering to creative play.

I bet you already have those creative juices flowing and can think of many other scenarios. I have experimented with a few ideas; I will share with you.

Frame Finishing and Frame Sizes

Frame Finishing

I often do not do anything to a frame and just leave them natural. For some sets I lightly stain them. For bases that we take outside I seal them with a clear varnish.

To stain a frame, just water down some acrylic paint and sponge or brush it on the interior of the frame.

Cloth Additions:

Sometimes I line the interior of a few frames with felt. It is easy to change out colors, gives doll furniture a little traction so they do not slide around when playing in the car and it can dampen the sound a bit of those peg dolls that walk a little heavy.

I also cut room rugs out of cotton scraps and use pinking shears to make a more finished looking edge that resists fraying. See the Living Room Rugs sections for details.

Footed Wood Serving Stand:

I have found raised serving trays on sale and have tried one or two as a playscape. They tend to be expensive for being such a simple construction.

You can make one out of pine by cutting a 1"x10" board to approx 12 inches. Round off the edges by sanding and glue on large candle cups as feet or even use a large square dowel or 2"x2" piece of wood for the legs.

Just some ideas for you to explore!

Play Ideas

If you've picked up this book, you are probably a pretty creative person, so I don't need to preach to the choir. But I do want to reinforce that you are on the correct path to enriching your child's play skills and imagination.

You are your child's first teacher. When playing with toddlers and younger children, model simple actions they are familiar with. The doll is hungry. Let's go to the kitchen to make food, the doll is sleepy, let's take a nap. We will read books and sing a song to our doll before bedtime. Oh let's not forget to brush our teeth!

As your child grows, ask them questions about the doll's character and what it likes to do, and help them create a story about the doll's adventures. I prefer to let the child lead, but to help increase quality and length of play, be ready with new ideas to introduce.

Leveling Up: Years 4-6 – Ideas for Expanding Play

Expanding Themes

When you expand your peg doll collection with additional play themes, you actually give new life to your child's existing peg doll toys giving them new energy and ideas. Expanding your collection also encourages increased focus. I found that while my grandchildren happily played with the current peg doll set, I could slowly be working on the next few additions. By the time I finished and presented them with a new set of accessories, they got a renewed joy and excitement for more creative play with the peg dolls they already had. This is similar to what educators do to stimulate play in their classroom. Children do not need a lot of toys. Quality toys matter more than quantity. Toys that can be used creatively together benefit children the most.

Planning New Sets

You can consider each room in this book as a small set. Start by making the level one toys first. Don't be afraid to let your child play with characters or new accessories as you complete them, your child will continue to build their imagination as they play with each new level of a set. As you observe their play, watch and listen. What your child is focusing on in their play will inform you what to craft next. Maybe your child is focusing on the kitchen and serving food. What food do they like? Think how you might add that to their play. See the DIY kitchen accessories for ideas too.

Include your older child in the toy making process. Have your child brainstorm with you, draw out items, or choose colors etc. You can substitute some screen time for toy making time several times a week. Since doll painting projects often require a base coat and some dry time, the pace is perfect for conversation and spending quality time with your children.

Resources

Peg Dolls

3½ inch dolls (female) - 3-1/2" Jumbo Angel - **Woodpeckers**
3½ inch dolls (male) - 3-1/2" Jumbo Dad - **Woodpeckers**
2 5/16 inch doll (child) - Woodpile Fun! Wood Peg Men – **Hobby Lobby**
1 inch dolls (toy doll) - 1" Wooden Peg People by **Creatology - Michaels**
1-1/8 inch dolls (toys) - 1-1/8" Baby Peg Dolls – **Woodpeckers**

Bedroom

No Build Bed: 5x3" wood plaque - **Michaels**
Beds: 4" coasters - **Michaels**
DIY Lamps bases: **Wood Finial Dowel Caps** – Hobby Lobby
1" Apples: **Woodpeckers Crafts**
Book box: Mayberry Street Miniatures Miniature Wood Cabinet With Drawers – **Hobby Lobby** books: **Square Wood Shapes**

Kitchen

Sink / Stove: 2" Square Wood Block by Make Market - Michaels
Table: 3" plaques
Table legs: 1" ball knobs

Kitchen accessories

Plates: **Hobby Lobby Wood Stack Checkers** - 1 1/4" Also at Woodpeckers Crafts
Bowls - **3/4" Wooden Miniature Bowl - Woodpeckers**
Glasses: Hobby Lobby Wood Candle cups
Cook / bean pot: Hobby Lobby Wood Candle cups
Pantry Jars - **Miniature Mason Jar, 3/4" - Woodpeckers**
Palumba:**Unfinished Dollhouse Wooden Miniature Accessory Set** - 70 plus pieces
Amazon: **HABA Little Friends Dollhouse Kitchen Accessories** – 24 pieces

Bathroom

Sink: 2" Square Wood Block by Make Market - Michaels
Tub: **Michaels small wood plaque**
Shower: 4" coasters rectangle and circle- Michaels
Shower head: **Wood Split Balls**
Shower knobs: **Wood Axle Dowel Caps With 1/4" Hole - 9/16"**
Child stool platform:
Child stool legs: **Wood Axle Dowel Caps With 1/4" Hole - 9/16"**

Living Room

Couch: 4" coasters rectangle (solid and welled)
Chair: 4" coasters rectangle (solid and welled)
Coffee table: craft wood at Home Depot or Lowes
Side table: craft wood at Home Depot or Lowes
TV: craft wood at Home Depot or Lowes
Radio: **Circle Wood Shapes**
Radio antenna: Bamboo Wood Dowels by Make Market - Michaels
Longcase or Floor clock face: **Circle Wood Shapes**
Vacuum: **Wood Tie Rack Pegs**
Floor Lamp: flower pots Woodpeckers
House plants: Hobby Lobby candle cups

Play Environments Frame sizes

Dollar Tree frame - square and rectangular in the Plus craft section. They do not require any modifications and are ready to be played with.
Michael's frame -**10" Square Wood Plaque by Make® Market** remove wall hanger

Hobby Lobby Curved Wood Wall Decor - remove wall hanger (Length: 13 11/16" Width: 23 3/4" Thickness: 3/4") I only have one of these since it is a little larger, but I like to offer a variety of shapes and sizes to supplement creativity.

Woodworking Tools

Band saw -
Drill Press - WEN 4208T 2.3-Amp 8-Inch 5-Speed Cast Iron Benchtop Drill Press
Drill Press Vice - WEN Drill Press Vise, 3-Inch
Drill bits -
Handheld router
Spindle Sander - WEN HA5932 5-Amp Variable Speed Portable Oscillating Spindle Sander
Wood Glue

About the Author

Emily Kellagher has a master's degree in education and has taught preschool, kindergarten, middle school science, and more.

Emily finds beauty, creativity, and fun in her daily life. She spends her time biking, creating, and dreaming up fun activities to enjoy with her grandchildren.

Growing up, Emily made natural dollhouses while camping using rocks, acorns, and sticks. She has shared her love of creative pretend play with her children, countless schoolchildren, and now her grandchildren. Her favorite material remains natural wood, which she uses to craft playscapes for peg dolls, showcasing her ingenuity and creativity.

"I want to inspire play for all ages with natural materials that spark the imagination, harness creativity, and promote sustainability."

www.emilykellagher.com
www.craftedjoypress.com

Join Our Peg Doll Toy Crafting Community

Become a Member! Share pictures of your creations with our Peg Doll Community. Chat with others. Be a part of exclusive author demos and talks. It is a secure platform. Or if you are on Instagram tag #craftedjoypress #pegdollhomes.

Free Download

I saved a special project for our community members.
Join and receive an extra project to create for your peg doll home.

https://emilykellagher.com/projects/gifts

Acknowledgments

♥ My wonderful, loving, patient, supportive husband who is a partner in toy creation. He patiently listens as I explain my ideas and will cut out pieces of wood to help bring my designs to life.

♥ My beautiful artistic daughter who painted all the peg dolls in this book for me. She is truly original in her artistic sensibilities. She is also always supportive, thank you.

♥ My granddaughters, who are energetic, creative and full of fun! I love playing with you and creating toys you enjoy.

Thanks for reading! Please add a short review on Amazon and let me know what you thought!

"If you enjoyed reading this, please leave a review on Amazon. I read every review, and they help new readers discover my books."

Visit **http://craftedjoypress.com** for more information about upcoming books, get our newsletter with other toy making ideas and download free supplemental peg doll accessory projects.

Crafted Joy Press